Time Critical

a play by Stan's Cafe

ISBN 978-1-913185-10-7

Published by Stan's Cafe
Birmingham, UK
2020

www.stanscafe.co.uk

Time Critical © Stan's Cafe 2017
Photos © Graeme Braidwood 2016
Publication © Stan's Cafe 2020

Extract from *The Carrier Frequency* text by Russell Hoban
With kind permission from the Russell Hoban Estate.

Extract from *Finger Trigger Bullet Gun* by Nenad Prokić
With kind permission from Nenad Prokić.

Contents:

Staging 1
Notes on the text 2
Time Critical 3
Bonus Material
Original Programme Notes 44

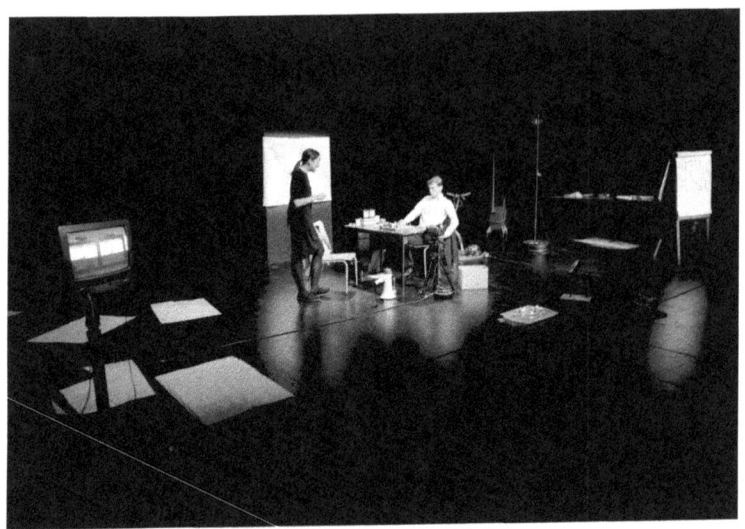

Staging

When seated the two performers face each other across a table. On the table is a chess board. When members of Stan's Cafe, their friends and relations are mentioned in the text, chess pieces are often added to, taken from or moved around the board in an approximate equivalent to the event referred to in the text.

Beside the board, upstage, facing the audience, is a chess clock with 26 minutes allocated to each player. A live relay to a television down stage right allows the audience to see the clock's twin faces in close up. Performers punch the clock to stop it counting down on their side and they make increasingly anxious references to the clock as they start running out of time.

Downstage left a flip chart stands waiting to count down years from 1991 to the present. Stage right a stack of hand drawn protest posters lie face down waiting to be held up to the audience.

Upstage of the table a single black flat has a large map of the world pinned to it, when performers mention place names or journeys they often mark them out on this map with a marker pen. For the tour of *Time Critical* we had a map designed bespoke for the show and a fresh copy printed for each performance that was then left behind as documentation of the performance.

Stage left stands a stationary bicycle from *Home Of The Wriggler* stands. Peddling this bicycle powers car headlights for a small section of this show.

The original production of *Time Critical* was made for Stan's Cafe's 25th Anniversary Party in 2016. This script is for the touring version remade a year later. Modest changes include adding Amy Ann Haigh's biographical strand as she took over performing from Rochi Rampal, most of whose biographical material stayed. With an extra year's worth of events to account for one minute was added to each side of the chess clock for this tour.

Notes On The Text

D – Director   A – Amy   C – Craig.

[ ] indicates a stage directions.

{ } indicates a sign protest being held up.

Amy holds up all protest signs unless stated.

-------XXXXXX------- indicates text on the flip chart.

Craig performs most of the flip chart flips.

/ Indicates speech that is cut off.

Lighting cues are included to give a sense of the show's focus.

Music cues are included as they are from the Stan's Cafe archive.

Section names are for reference and are not part of the script.

--**Time Critical**--

> *[LX 1: Preset = house flip chart and map]*
> *[LX1.5: Intro General]*

Formation of Stan's Cafe

D: *[Semi-improvised]* Welcome everyone to Time Critical, we are glad you could make it. My name is James and I'm here to quickly explain how this show works as it's slightly unusual. Now we feel we can guarantee you fifty two minutes of entertainment in the show, but we can't promise to get to the end of the script as our two performers will be under a bit of time pressure. Let me introduce them to you.

First of all, representing the whole world, on my right Amy Anne Haigh *[A enters]* and on my left, representing Stan's Cafe, Craig Stephens.

The rules are simple, you each have twenty six minutes to cover your half of the story. Craig, twenty six years of Stan's Cafe, Amy, twenty six years of everything else. Punch the clock when you have done your bit and the other person's clock will start counting down.

Are you ready?

A Yes.

C *[Flips the flip chart]*

--**1991**--

[Sits] Yes.

D Then on your marks, get set, go!
   [Punches clock so C's side starts counting down]

	[LX 2: Scene]
C:	Graeme, I know you probably won't, because it's so soon after Glory What Glory broke up and you probably don't want to get yourself back into that kind of thing, but I wonder if maybe you'd like to start a theatre company with me?
A:	Oh, ah, that sounds great, yes, why not?
C:	Yes! Excellent. *[C punch clock]*
	[LX 3: General]
A:	Soviet troops storm the TV tower in Vilnius, Lithuania. Coalition forces bomb Iraq starting operation Desert Storm. Iraq bombs Israel and invades Saudi Arabia. The IRA launch a mortar bomb attack on 10 Downing Street while John Major is meeting with thee cabinet members to discuss the gulf war – one of the bombs lands in the back garden. US troops cross into Kuwait. Iraqi forces set fire to oil wells as they leave. There are mass protests in Belgrade against the rule of Slobodan Milosevic. {Be human, leave now!} Soviet forces attack border posts in Lithuania. Latvians set up barricades around bridges and important buildings in Riga. The Yugoslav People's Army advances towards Slovenia. Slovenia's government takes control of border posts and airport.
C:	Graeme and James move into 85 Ombersley Road, Balsall Heath, Birmingham and start rehearsing in the front room. I finish my MA, move to London and get a job unloading boxes of books.
A:	Soldiers of the YPA advance on Dubrovnik and destroy water and electricity supplies. The city is bombarded and under siege until the following year. Gorbachev is put under house arrest whilst on holiday.

Gorbachov Under House Arrest.

[LX 4: Close to table.]

A:	*[Playing chess]* "Right, another beautifully orchestrated strategic victory for me I believe. Now, let's get back to Moscow".

C:	"We cannot advise that. You will be much safer here in your Dacha in Crimea".
A:	"Safer? Safer from what?"
C:	"Those who may not be as excited about Glasnost as you".
A:	"As me? What about you? What happened to us?"
C:	"Another game Comrade Gorbachov?"
A:	Nice accent!
C:	We should do more.
	[LX 5: General]
A:	Thousands protest against this coup. Boris Yeltsin makes a speech on a tank. *[Stands on table]*

"Citizens of Russia: On the night of 18-19 August 1991, the legally elected president of the country was removed from power. Regardless of the reasons given for his removal, we are dealing with a rightist, reactionary, anti-constitutional coup."

The coup collapses and Gorbachev returns to power – he dissolves the Central Committee of the Communist Party ending Communist rule.

The Soviet flag is lowered for the last time.
Two days later Yeltsin moves into Gorbachev's office and I eat jelly at my third Birthday party. *[A punch clock]*

C: You're THREE?

---1992---

Memoirs of an Amnesiac

[Music: Desespoire Agreable from Memoirs Of An Amnesiac]
[LX 6: Stan's Cafe state on Craig]

C: "Yes, she works on the ground floor and I work on the third floor, that's where all the work that I do is done, so we don't see each other that often. That is unless we happen to bump into each other on the stairwell, if I'm going down to the basement where the photostat machine is and if she is going up to the second floor. That's where her friends work, on the second floor. She sometimes goes up to the fourth floor where the canteen is but no, I never go to the canteen because people always look at you, sitting on your own and

think that you don't want to be on your own when in fact you do want to be on your own and they get embarrassed and I don't like to see that, so I don't eat in the canteen. I eat my sandwiches elsewhere. Mmmm…" *[C punch clock] [Music: out] [LX 7: General]*
Graeme works at the Northfield Benefits office while James mops floors as a kitchen porter, in the evenings they devise *Memoirs of An Amnesiac.*

A: George H.W. Bush is sick in the lap of the Japanese Prime Minister.
Boris Yeltsin and George Bush agree to stop targeting each other with nuclear weapons.
Bosnian Serbs declare their own independent republic within Bosnia and Herzegovina.
Bosnia and Herzegovina declares independence from Yugoslavia.
The army of the Republic of Serbia begins a long siege of Sarajevo.
EuroDisney opens.
Stephen Lawrence is killed.
In LA police officers are acquitted of using excessive force in the arrest of Rodney King {We can all get along} leading to six days of protests and riots across the city.
John Major wins the UK election.
The pound and the lira are forced out of the European Exchange rate Mechanism.
There is a bomb at the Baltic Exchange.
Bill Clinton is on the campaign trail in the USA.
[LX 7.5: Speech spot]
"For millions and millions of Americans the dream with which I grew up has been shattered. We're divided by race and region by income, by age and gender. We are all cut up. The beginning of everything is believing that we can do better"
[LX 7.6: General]
The ANC call a general strike {We stand by our leaders} in South Africa in protest at the lack of progress in negotiations with the government.
Bill Clinton is elected president.
In Berlin and Rostock thousands protest against attacks on immigrants. {Racism Kills} *[A punch clock]*

C: Fifteen years later Stan's Cafe is in Rostock performing on the fringes of the G8 conference. *[C holds poster]* {G8 stop talking act now} *[C punch clock]*
A: The separation of Charles and Diana is announced. *[A punch clock]*

---1993---

Canute the King #1

[Music: Corridor Music from Canute The King]
[LX 8: Stan's Cafe state DS]
[A & C light candles in the bows of tin foil boats before naming and launching the boats on a try full of water]

C: "I name this ship Voice of Stars".
A: "I name this ship Fortune (favouring the brave)".
C: "I name this ship Cheap but Sturdy".
A: "I name this ship Pure of Heart".
C: "I name this ship Drifting Never Lost".

"So here I am looking out at the sea,
we'll call it the sea for today.
Down there are my gardens,
my fine trees and hedges,
for now I'll call it the sea".

"I hear the waves as brown leaves blown by wind,
see only black oil, the scum and the floatings.
I try to hold it all as I did in the past,
but this time it's stronger than me".

"Time still passing, marked off on the marble, climbing the stairs.
Sunday, I wonder the number of times we've been dreaming,
Sunday, still no sign of the turning". *[C punch Clock]*
[LX 8.5: Table light]

A: "I consider it immensely important that we concern ourselves with culture. Not just as one among many human activities but in the broader scene the culture of everything. The general level of public manners. By that I chiefly mean the relations that exist among people, between the powerful and the weak, the healthy and the sick".
[LX 9: General]
C: I know that, it's the playwright Vaclev Havel. *[Exits]*
[Music: fade out]
A: Czechoslovakia splits into the Czech Republic and Slovakia in a velvet divorce. The president of the Czech Republic is Vaclev Havel. *[A punch clock]*

It's Your Film and the Roma.

C: *[Enter carrying box]* Seven years later we're in the Czech Republic performing *It's Your Film* in Prague, Kölin and a small town, Litvinov on the boarder with the former East Germany.
A: "Hello"
C: "Hello, dobri den"
A: "You have show here?"
C: "Yes tomorrow, we're just setting up today"
A: "Sexy show?"
C: "Well, good, it's a good show, maybe not sexy"
A: "Peepshow"
C: "Well, there is a viewing booth, you see the show is just four and a half minutes long and…"
A: "You are Ladyboy!"
C: "No, I'm not an err Lady Boy I err"
A: "Do not worry. They hate us too. The Czech hate us"

C: "Really, is that the case?"
A: "We are Roma, you know Roma?"
C: "Yes, we are aware of the err Roma/"
A: "/Everyone hates us"
C: "We'll I'm sure they don't/"
A: "We are niggers of Europe"
C: *[C punch clock]* That was getting a bit uncomfortable.

A: Trade barriers are brought down as the European Single Market is set up.
The International Criminal Tribunal for Yugoslavia is set up.
The Taylor family win a holiday in Euro Disney courtesy of *This Morning* – a television program hosted by Richard and Judy.
C: They're supposed to be world events!
A: Bill Clinton is inaugurated as President of the USA.
A bomb explodes outside the World Trade Center in New York and another bomb explodes at Bishopsgate in the City of London and the Shankhill Road in Belfast and there is a mass shooting at Greysteel, county Londonderry.
All Soviet troops finally leave Poland, waved goodbye by the former electrician and union official, now president, Lech Walesa.
Benazir Bhutto is elected as Prime Minister of Pakistan for the second time.
The Mount Carmel Center near Waco in Texas is under siege by FBI Agents for 51 days: *[C under the table]*
[LX 10: Tight to table & under table].

A: *[With megaphone walking round table]* "Individuals inside the Branch Davidian compound we are in the process of placing tear gas into the building this is not an assault, this is not an assault, we will not be entering the building. This is not an assault."
[LX 11: General]

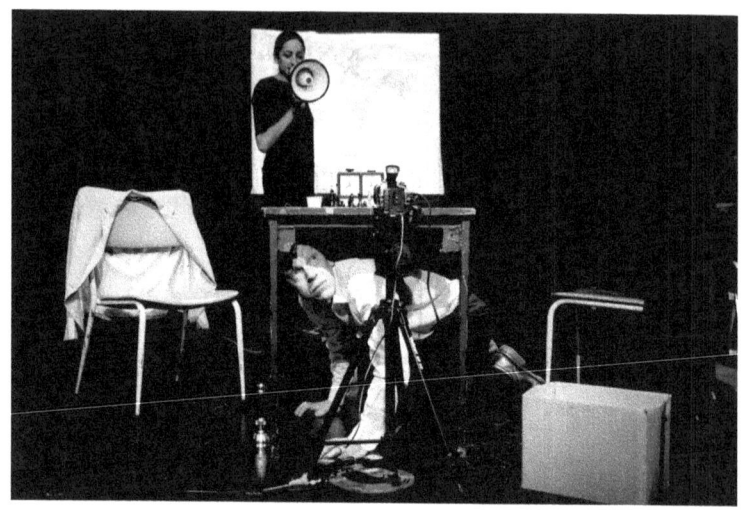

-----1994-----

C: *[C punch clock]*
    James splits up with his long time girlfriend for the final time and moves into a bedsit on Park Hill. Graeme rents a room from his mates Nick and Vikki. *[C punch clock]*

A: A man fires blanks at Prince Charles in Australia. *[C dives under desk]*
    A mortar shell kills many people in a market place in Sarajevo.
    The Scream is stolen in Oslo; then found again.
    Police begin excavating a house at Cromwell Street in Gloucester.
    China gets its first internet connection.
    The Church of England ordains its first female priests.
    Silvio Berlusconi wins the presidential election in Italy and hundreds of thousands of people are killed in Rwanda.
    There is a ceasefire in the Balkans but only for a few days.
    O.J.Simpson flees slowly from police in a white Ford Bronco.
    An electrician discovers the body of Kurt Cobain at the singer's home in Seattle.
    There are elections in South Africa and Nelson Mandela becomes president.

[LX 11.5: Speech spot]
"Your Majesties, Your Highnesses, Distinguished Guests, Comrades and Friends…"
[LX 11.6: General] [C punch clock]

A: More work needed on the accent?
C: It is slightly offensive.
In Paris late at night members of Stan's Cafe are in the back of a large, sleek back car speeding through the Pont de l'Alma tunnel, they are drunk on red wine, the car is driving too fast. [C punch clock]
A: On the Imola race track in Italy Ayrton Senna crashes and is killed.
Francois Mitterand and Queen Elizabeth II get on trains and meet up in Calais to officially open the Channel Tunnel.
C: [Shaking hands under the table] "Hello"
A: "Bonjour"
[To map] The last Russian troops leave Germany .
After 49 years the last allied troops leave Berlin.
There are protests against Castro's government in Cuba.
The IRA announces a complete cessation of military operations.
Russia and China stop pointing their nuclear weapons at each other.
Construction begins on the Three Gorges Dam.
A jet is hijacked in Marseilles.
AOL provided a dial up service to the web for the American public.
The National Lottery is born.
C: Hooray.
A: Justin Bieber is born.
C: Hooray.
A: Telly Savalas dies.
C: Boo.
A: *Friends* starts.
C: Hooray.

---**1995**---

A: The trial of OJ Simpson begins:
[LX 11.7: Speech Spot]
"It's my opportunity, it's my honour and privilege, on behalf of the defence, and our defence team, as it were, to stand

	before you now and address you in what is called an opening statement."
C:	Do you really want to do this?
A:	Yes.
	"Now, the opening statement is not an opening argument, but it's just that: an opening statement."
C:	It's just you've got a lot to cover and I'm not sure the opening statement from the O.J.Simpson trial is a high priority, is it?
A:	I want to do it. It's my time. I've learnt it. I'll do it.
	"Now, the opening statement is not an opening argum/"
	[C punch clock]
	[LX 11.8: General]
C:	O.J.Simpson is found not guilty.
	Ebay is founded.
	The Yahoo search engine is launched but Stan's Cafe is not online. *[C punch clock]*
A:	There is war in Chechnya.
	The Army of the Republic Of Serbia led by Ratko Mladic moves into Srebrenica and kills thousands of Muslim Bosniak men and boys.
	NATO begins bombing Bosnian Serb positions in Bosnia and Herzegovina.
	The Schengen Agreement comes into force.
C:	Hooray.
A:	The DVD is born.
C:	Hooray.
A:	The Dayton Agreement is signed bringing an end to the Bosnian war. *[Paper signed]*
C:	Hooray.
A:	Louis Farrakhan is joined by a million men marching in Washington DC.
	Steve Fossett flies solo across the pacific in a balloon.
	Yitzhak Rabin is assassinated.
	Nick Leeson breaks Barings Bank.
	A bomb is set off in Oklahoma.

Voodoo City #1
[Music: String Quartet from Voodoo City]
[LX 12: Stan state DS.]

C: "And this city renounces sleep for fear of its dreams,
This city renounces its right to rest for fear of falling apart,
This city renounces sleep and rest and giving of room for thoughts for fear or chance of streets and devils turning in on themselves.
And we renounce it all, our right to darkness, sleep or rest or hope or giving room to thoughts or anything that might be seen as old or gone or spent or dust,
for chance that thoughts turn in and spiralling from the city that spewed us up, than that its turning thoughts left unpropelled by whirlwind city turning and flying trains gliding past, covered by the kill cat rattle of drop dead lorry driven round this
big city, big city, big place lost place and homesick land. And this is how we make this spell and spell this spell and this is how we raise the sleeping dead of suburb land."
[C punch clock]
[LX 13: General]

---**1996**---

A: Bombs explode in Canary Wharf, Manchester and Enniskillen.
[Music out]
In a school in Dunblane sixteen children and their teacher are shot by a gunman, 10 year old Jamie and 9 year old Andy Murray escape unharmed.
The Sea Empress hits rocks on its way to Milford Haven and spills 72,000 tonnes of crude oil into the sea.
The European Union bans exports of British beef.
The PLO drops its call for the eradication of Israel.
Israel reciprocates.
UN weapons inspectors look for weapons of mass destruction in Iraq. *[A punch clock]*

C: Feeling squeezed out of Stan's Cafe Graeme leaves with composer Richard Chew to form The Resurrectionists. After deciding I should get a proper job I start a PGCE. James drives to Stockport to meet Nina West and her partner Jane. He's heard Nina's music at a party and thinks she would do a great job creating a soundtrack for the next Stan's Cafe show. She does.

Ocean of Storms #1

[Music: It's Your Film section of Ocean of Storms Soundtrack + Tie Clip Microphones]
[LX 14: Stan's Cafe state]

C: "Trafalgar Road, Alfred Road, Britain. New fake old furniture. Flake paint window sill. Window too dirty to see through"
A: "Hello Caroline"
C: "Total mystery land now"
A: "Yeah it's me"
C: "47"
A: "I just wondered"
C: "48 on the lamp posts"
A: "Can you come over?"
C: "50"
A: "Only I've got something to tell you. No it's important you've go to come over. No I can't tell you on the phone. It's just really stupid that's all. No just really dumb. I've taken a lot of pills Caroline"
C: "Broken sign"
A: "Oh I don't know too many"
C: "Alfred road"
A: "About an hour ago, only, I don't feel so good now, no I'm beginning to feel a bit sick, dizzy. Will you come over?"
C: "Hello service control how can we help you?"
A: "Only I wish I hadn't done it now"
C: "That shouldn't be a problem at all"
A: "I feel dizzy"
C: "We should have some one with you within thirty minutes"
A: "Can you come over?"
C: "You're welcome"

[C punch clock]
[Music: out and microphones out]
[LX 15: General]

A: *[At map]* There is a ceasefire in the war in Chechnya.
The Nintendo 64 is released.
C: Hooray.
A: Dolly the Sheep is cloned.
C: Hooray.
A: The Ramones play their last gig.
C: Boo.
A: Deep Blue beats Kasparov.
Villa win the League Cup.

C: Hooray.
A: Amy Taylor plays Louisa in *The Sound Of Music* at Stourbridge Town Hall.
Hotmail is launched.
C: Stan's Cafe aren't yet online.
A: Ella Fitzgerald dies.

---**1997**---

A: Work begins on repairing the Hubble Space Telescope.
Divorce becomes legal in the Republic of Ireland.
{Divorce Kills Families}
C: Really!
A: Comet Hale Bopp passes over the earth.
"Things can only get better"
Labour take power in the UK. Tony Blair becomes PM .
C: Hooray.
A: The UK wins the Eurovision Song Contest.
C: Hooray.
A: Timothy McVeigh convicted for his role in 1995 Oklahoma bombing

J.K.Rowling #1 In Cafe.
[LX 16: closer on table]
A: "Hello"
C: "Aye?"
A: "Well I wonder if you're thinking of buying another coffee? You've been nursing that one for a wee while now"
C: "Well I'm a single mother aren't I, I canee afford ta be spendin' all day buying cappuccinos canna?"
A: "Well I understand that be we are busy and if you aren't/"
C: "/arm in the last stages of writing my first novel fur children about a wee wizard boy at wizard school, I canna be distracted"
A: "I do appreciate that but we do have a business"
C: "What? Are yer kickin me oot? I'll show youz, this is gonna be fuckin' massive, I'm gonna earn millions and I'm gonna buy this fuckin' Elephant Hoos fuckin' cafe and when I do you are gonna be oot of a fuckin' job sonny"
[LX 17: General]
A: *Harry Potter and the Philosopher's Stone* is published
and Hong Kong is handed over to China.

C:	Hooray.
A:	*[A punch Clock]*
C:	An eighteen year old Rochi Rampal and a fifteen year old Jack Trow devise *No Walls Just Doors* with Stan's Cafe as part of Stage 2 youth theatre. James buys a house on Runcorn Road. Nick Walker moves in. Meanwhile, in Luton, while I'm opening a letter inviting me to an interview for a teaching job, the phone goes. "Hello"
A:	"Hello it's James from Stan's Cafe"
C:	"Oh hi James"
A:	"I just wondered if you fancied being in our new show *Simple Maths*"
C:	"Yeah, absolutely" *[Tears letter to confetti and throws it]* *[Music: From Simple Maths]* *[LX 17.5: Stan's Cafe state slow fade]*
C:	*[As if a chess game]* Nick, Sarah, Jake, Amanda, and Craig Stephens, sit next to each other on five of six chairs. Nick moves to the spare chair.
A:	Sarah stands up and moves to the chair that Nick has just left.
C:	Jake stands up and sits back down again without changing chairs.
A:	Amanda moves to Sarah's old chair and starts smiling.
C:	I stand up, sit down and start yawning.
A:	Nick moves to Amanda's old chair and starts looking anxious.
C:	Etc. etc. this continues for about an hour. *[Music: Off]*

Simple Maths Argument.

[LX 18: Stan's Cafe General]

A:	"Excuse me, are you the director of that show?"
C:	"Simple Maths? Yes, actually, I am"
A:	"Well I thought it was the worst show I've ever seen, nothing/"
C:	/she didn't say that.
A:	It's what she was thinking!
C:	You can't say the subtext, that's the whole point of subtext, it's under the text. What she actually said was. "I went to drama school and the first thing they taught us was that theatre is all about conflict"
A:	"And there was no conflict in that nothing happened, it was

	so boring"
C:	"Well there was actually you weren't looking care/"
A:	"/at just went on and on and nothing happened/"
C:	They don't need to hear this. *[C punch clock].*

[LX 19: Speech spot]
[Music: Turning the Tide from Canute The King]

A: "We are today a nation in a state of shock, in mourning, in grief that is so deeply painful for us. She was the People's Princess and that is how she will stay, how she will remain in our hearts and our memories for ever."

Canute the King #2 Di Death.

[LX 20: Stan's Cafe DS]

C: *[C punch clock]*
"History's seas are rising up embracing us to take us home.
So down you lie and down you lie
the shells all sing to take you in
and cradle you in finest sand of hour-glass quartz
and powder you in mica,
to drape you in a filigree silt of love and guilt
which washes from all the bedrock books of yore.

Once sea now land now sea once more
Once sea now land now sea once more"

[A punch clock]
[LX 20.5: General]

A: In Pakistan a daughter is born to Mr. & Mrs. Yousafzai.

---**1998**---

War begins in Kosovo.
Meanwhile in Northern Ireland:
"We, the participants in the multi-party negotiations, believe that the agreement we have negotiated offers a truly historic opportunity for a new beginning. The tragedies of the past have left a deep and profoundly regrettable legacy of suffering. We are committed to partnership, equality and mutual respect as the basis of relationships within Northern Ireland, between North and

	South, and between these islands"
	The Good Friday agreement is signed.
C:	Hooray.
	[LX 21: General] [Music: out]
A:	France win the World Cup.
C:	Hooray.
A:	A bomb goes off in Omagh. *[C dives for table]*
	Google is founded.
C:	Hooray.
	Stan's Cafe get dial up internet access. *[C punch clock]*
	Their email address is admin@stanscafe.force9.co.uk
A:	Hooray.
C:	Thank you.
	I buy a pager and my bike is stolen from outside Birmingham REP
	[C punch Clock]
A:	Work starts on building the Large Hadron Collider at CERN.
C:	Hooray.
A:	India and Pakistan test nuclear weapons. *[A punch clock]*

---**1999**--

Carrier Frequency #1.

[Music: Carrier Frequency Track 2]
[LX 22: Stan's Cafe]

A: Woyomean?

C: Meanwa Isay doan I. If nat Osostrong Earny Warling lissen lissen alla time nyan day wy he din stop nat fuckin boomboom badstuff wy he din stop nem bigbig megatonsya? Wy he din stop nat Osodreadful wa Im gonna say. Im gonna say nat Osodreadful name.

A: Ono doansay nat osodreadful name O pleasy pleasy doan say nat.

C: Doan wan sayit but iss comin up in me like I ga puke. Iss comin up in me I canstop it. I gon puke it out iss comin now.

A: Ono O plasy pleasy pleasy pleasy doan puke it.
[Music: out]
[LX 23: General]

C: Mark Anderson reinforces this table for Stan's Cafe's revival of Impact Theatre's show The Carrier Frequency made in collaboration with the novelist Russell Hoban. Mr. Hoban

	visits the production and calls the company 'luvvies', but in a nice way. Graeme Rose returns to Stan's Cafe for this production and subsequent touring of *It's Your Film*. *[C punches clock]* I am given my first mobile phone.
A:	And so am I.
C:	*[Craig does a double take]*

A: Bill Clinton's impeachment trial begins and ends with him being acquitted.
Bertrand Piccard and Brian Jones become first people to circumnavigate the globe non-stop in a hot air balloon.
[C takes a plastic cup from the table as a model balloon basket]
Wait! It takes them just under 20 days *[C slows down]*.
NATO launch airstrikes against Belgrade and the Yugoslav military in response to Yugoslav actions in the Kosovo war. Later in the year a peace treaty is signed and Yugoslav troops withdraw from Kosovo.
Bill Gates becomes richest person in the world.
Twelve students and a teacher are killed in Columbine High School.
There are elections in Wales and Scotland for the Welsh Assembly and the Scottish parliament.
Rehearsals for *Jack and the Beanstalk* by Stourbridge Pantomime Company are interrupted by a solar eclipse.
The Last Supper is placed back on display after 22 years of restoration.
MSN Messenger launched.
There are protests in Belgrade demanding the resignation of Milosevic.
The last Russian soldiers leave the Baltic states.
The Population of the world reaches six billion.
[A punch clock]

C: I move into Runcorn Road. Nick Walker moves out to live with Ann in Coventry. *[C sprinkles rice on chess board]*
A: What are they?
C: Rats, they've moved into the kitchen and they're living in my car.
A: Really?
C: Yes, they chew through the electrical cables and kill the engine in the middle lane of the A34 on the way to the Isle

	of Wight.
A:	What are you doing going to the Isle of Wight?
C:	To visit my girlfriend's parents.
A:	Your girlfriend?
C:	Charlotte Goodwin.
A:	Why've you not mentioned her?
C:	I've only just met her!
A:	And that wasn't worth mentioning?
C:	I didn't say that, look I've not got time for this!
	[C punch clock]
A:	5, 4 ,3 ,2,1.

---**2000**--

A:	….the millennium dome opens!
C:	And a day later The Black Maze opens at the ICC in Birmingham.
A:	Former KGB officer Vladimir Putin becomes President of Russia Having survived the Millennium Bug millions of computers are infected with the I Love You computer worm.
C:	Boo.
A:	The billionth living person in India is born.
C:	Hooray.
A:	The 5 mile long Oresund Bridge linking Denmark and Sweden is opened to traffic.
C:	Hooray.
A:	Milosevic resigns as President of Serbia.
C:	Hooray.
A:	Bashar Al Assad becomes Syria's leader in a referendum after the death of his father.
C:	Hooray.
A:	The last mini, a red one, comes off the production line at Longbridge.
C:	Hooray.
A:	MG Rover is sold by BMW to the Phoenix Consortium for £10.00.
C:	Hooray.
A:	Demolition of the old Bull Ring shopping centre in Birmingham. *[Putting rice grains in the plastic cup held up high]* William Shepherd, Yuri Gidzenko and Sergei Krikalev are

the first people to live on the International Space Station, Meanwhile, *[hiding grains of rice on table under upturned plastic cup]* ten people enter a house and are watched seven days a week for two months on Channel Four.
[A punch clock]

Good and True.
[LX 24: Stan's Cafe at table]

- C: "Do you recognise this?"
- A: "It's a house."
- C: "Of course it's a house, whose house is it Joanne?"
- A: "Don't know"
- C: "Yours, it's your house."
- A: "It's not"
- C: "Don't try to deny it"
- A: "It's not, there's no front door."
- C: "Oh you're right. okay hang on, bear with me. Right do you recognise this?"
- A: "That's my house!"
- C: "Exactly 62 Walford Drive, 9.30 last night, so where are you?"
- A: "I'm at the window"
- C: "No you're... oh. No no, that's supposed to be Shaun, it's too tall for you"
- A: "It's not Shaun. Shaun's got dark curly hair"
- C: "Oh I'm rubbish at this"
- A: "Well it's easy you've put the front door on so just draw some curtains in to cover me up or something"
- C: "Will, will that work?"
- A: "If you do it neatly no one will know"
- C: "I will"
- A: "You'll have to forget"
- C: "What's that?"
- A: "It's like this but later"

[LX 25: General]

---2001---

C: Graeme's son Archie is born. *[C punch clock]*
A: Wikipedia launches. *[A punch clock]*
C: I buy a house on Ashbrook Road with Charlotte Goodwin my Girlfriend. *[C punch clock]*
A: George W Bush becomes president. *[A punch clock]*
C: Stan's Cafe move into their own rehearsal space on New Canal Street, trains roll past the windows and we can climb onto the roof to survey the city. *[C punch clock]*
A: There is a Foot And Mouth outbreak in the UK, more than ten million cows and sheep were killed and burnt. *[A punch clock]*
C: Stan's Cafe perform *Lurid and Insane*, a rock musical in a farmers barn in Lancashire. *[C punch clock]*

9/11

[Music: Comfort Hour]
[LX 26: Acted scene]

A: "A girl got a pet goat. She liked to go running with her pet goat. She played with her goat in her house. She played with the goat in her yard. But the goat did some things that made the girl's dad mad. the goat ate things. he ate cans

and he ate canes. he ate pans.
[C comes in and whispers in A's ear – pause]
One day her dad said, "that goat must go. He eats too many things.""
[LX 27: General]

C: Muslims are spat at on the streets of Birmingham, London, Liverpool, Manchester, across Europe and North America. *Comfort Hour* is played every night on People's Radio Freedom.
[Music: Out]
A: US and UK forces launch operation Enduring Freedom in Afghanistan.
The IRA commences disarmament.
C: Hooray.
A: The iPod is launched with 5Gb of memory and a thousand songs in your pocket.
C: Hooray.
A: Enron files for bankruptcy.
C: Boo.
A: In Argentina long queues form at banks and cashpoints as restrictions are placed on cash withdrawals – this fuels unrest and protests . {No more Banks Thieves}
*[Craig enters wearing a ruff] W*hat are you doing?
C: Financial Crisis.
A: No, that one's later!

---**2002**---

R Euro notes and coins are introduced and replace the currencies of twelve European countries.
C: Hooray.
A: It's the Queen's Golden Jubilee {Luvlee Jublee}
C: Hooray. *[C punch clock]*
It's Your Film tours to Lisbon, Leipzig, Rio, Bexhill, St. Etienne, Zagreb, Rakvere, Vilnius, Douai, Dieppe and Belgrade.
As we drive into Belgrade the scars of NATO bombing are still visible. In the theatre an elderly lady visits, she gives us each a red rose
A: "Thank you for coming to our country."
C: The security guy on stage door spends all day watching the Milosevic's Trial on TV, he is charged with:

A: "genocide; complicity in genocide; deportation; murder; persecutions on political, racial or religious grounds; inhumane acts/forcible transfer"

C: Stan's Cafe are taken to a restaurant in the hills outside the city by the promoter and former playwright Nenad Prokić.

Nenad in Restaurant.
[LX 28: Fictional scene]
C: "Mmm delicious food, Nenad"
A: "Yes, it is isn't it this is one of my favourite restaurants [etc]/"
C: "Great wine too"
A: "Yes, delicious. Did you know they grow the grape...
[C silently hurries her up]
Could you pass the salt please?"
C: He says how much he likes the show.
A: "I like your show... a lot, yes, great show James"
C: He asks if we know his favourite book.
A: "Do you know my favourite book?"
C: It's called.
A: "It's called"
C: The Anatomy of Melancholy.
A: "The Anatomy of Melancholy"
C: By Robert Burton.
A: "By Richard Burton"
C: Robert
A: "Robert Burton. Do you know it?"
C: No.
A: "You ignoramus! That book is genius!"
C: He didn't say that he said "It's a great book"
A: "It's a great book. You should look it up when you get home"
C: "I will"
A: "You are the only company I could imagine adapting it for the stage"
C: "That's kind of you to say, of course I'll look it up and get a copy as soon as I get home"
[LX 29: General]
C *[Takes a copy of The Anatomy Of Melancholy out of a box]*
"Oh for heavens sake!" *[C punch clock]*

A: War continues in Afghanistan.
Eight hundred and fifty people are taken hostage for three

days in the the House of Culture of State Ball-Bearing Plant Number 1 in Dubrovka Theatre in Moscow by Chechens demanding an end to the second Chechen war.

"We have nothing to lose. We have already covered two thousand kilometres by coming here. There is no way back... We have come to die. Our motto is freedom and paradise. We already have freedom as we've come to Moscow. Now we want to be in paradise."

C: *[C punch clock]* Amanda, Sarah and a student placement called Paula spend three days dressed as astronauts on a new fake station added to the Wolverhampton – Birmingham Metro line.
A: Why?
C: Art. *[C punch clock]*

A: UN Security Council Resolution 1441 is drawn up and adopted. Weapons inspector Hans Blix and his team are flown to Iraq.

Carrier Frequency #2 (reprise)
[Music: Carrier Frequency Track 2]
[LX 30: Stan's Cafe at table]
C: [Punch clock] "Erny Warling, Oso wuzza graybig lulabloak Osobigya Osostrong nor nat ain allno, Erny lissen alla noogy boogy alla time. Graybig Osobig ears he ga Erny. O my fingy wucha sucha graybig ears he ga ears he cud hear a fuckin fishfart downa bommna deep deep sea"
[Music: out]
[LX 31: General]
A: *[Punch clock]* Switzerland joins the United Nations after a referendum supporting membership.
C: Really?
A: Yep, they rejected joining in 1986.

C: *[C punch clock]* In June Zagreb sees its first Gay Pride march. Stan's Cafe are in town performing It's Your Film and join in to show solidarity. {Gays to the Camps}
A: What!
C: No, that's not us, that's the crowd, one of the fascists in the crowd, who do you think we are?

---**2003**---

Ocean of Storms #2 (reprise)
[Music: It's Your Film section of Ocean of Storms & tie clip microphones]
[LX 32: Stan's Cafe]

A: "Welcome to The Late Show and if you've just joined us here, we've got a caller on line 3. What's your name?"
C: "Hello CapCom, this is Ocean Rider"
A: "...and do you have a message for anyone out there tonight?"
C: "It's cold up here"
A: "That's really beautiful Andrew if you're listening out there, she loves you very much"
C: "I'm losing power"
A: "Do you have any requests?"
C: "I need a guidance report urgently"
A: "Well we'll see what we can do and meanwhile if there's anyone out there with a special message call us now"
C: "Ocean Rider to CapCom, I'm losing you, come in Al"
[LX 33: Slow fade to general]
[Music: slow fade out]
A: "Columbia, Houston UHF comm check
[C punch clock]
Flight GC, no band hits
Copy
Columbia, Houston, UHF comm check"

C: *[C punch clock]* Zoran Dindic who became the Prime Minister of Serbia in 2001 after the overthrow of Milosevic is assassinated under orders of a former secret police command, he is shot while getting out of his car at Serbian government buildings in Belgrade.
A: This is on your time, is that okay?
C: Nenad Prokić, a friend of Dindic, forms the Serbian Liberal Democratic Party.
[C punches clock]

It's Your Film in Skopje
A: War begins in Darfur.
Over one February weekend millions of people protest in cities across the world against an imminent war with Iraq.

	{Stop The War} *[A punch clock]*
C:	In Skopje this advice comes through to Stan's Cafe.
	[Music: Hex from Voodoo City]
	[LX 34: acted scene]
A:	"The Foreign Office are recommending all British Nationals keep a low profile"
C:	"But we've been doing interviews ever since we got here, TV, radio the works"
A:	"Yes, the official line is that you should cancel your shows"
C:	"Really?"
A:	"I'm just telling you what I've been told to tell you"
C:	"What do you think we should do?"
A:	"It's not for me to say I'm afraid. That's your decision to make"
C:	"Well I suppose it's only one audience member at a time"
A:	"Exactly and there'll be an armed guard on the door anyway"
C:	"Yeah! Ay, will there?" *[C punch clock]*
	[LX 35: General]
A:	Iraq is invaded by a US led coalition using shock and awe.
C:	The boom boom hard stuff.
A:	Coalition forces reach Baghdad, Saddam Hussein is overthrown and soon captured. *[Pulled out from under table]* *[A punch clock]*
	[Music: X fade to My Name Is… from Be Proud Of Me]
	[LX 36: Stan's Cafe Scene]

Be Proud of Me.

A:	"Open your mouth"
C:	"I have a heart condition"
A:	"Put out your tongue"
C:	"My nose keeps bleeding"
A:	"Please stand up. *[A listens to Cs chest]*
	Breathe in"
C:	"I have earache"
A:	"Hold your breath *[A lets C go]*
	I'll have to have a blood specimen
	What medicines are you taking?"
C:	"I take this medicine, could you give me another prescription?"
	[A puts magazine into gun]
A:	"I'll give you an antibiotic / a pain killer/ a sedative

	Take these pills / this medicine.
	Take this three times a day
	Take this to the chemist
	I'll give you an injection
	Roll up your sleeve"
	[C rolls up sleeve and puts arm on table]
C:	"I have difficulty in breathing"
	[A puts gun in C's hand]
A:	"The nerve is exposed, the tooth must be extracted. Come and see me in two days/a weeks time"
C:	"I feel sick, I feel dizzy"
	[C punch clock]
	[Music: Out]
	[LX 37: general]
A:	The human genome project is completed.
C:	Hooray.
	Jacob Rose is born.
A:	The new Bull Ring is opened.
	[A punch Clock]
C:	Three hundred thousand people visit on first day. Stan's Cafe premiere their soon to be acclaimed performance installation *Of All The People In All The World* at Warwick Arts Centre. This installation converts human population statistics into rice. Placing the rice on labelled piles sheets of paper one grain per person, Simon and Garfunkel. While performing in the Vancouver an audience member asks:
A:	"Is that really them?"
	[C punch clock]
A:	Concorde makes its last flight.
C:	Hooray.
A:	*[A punch clock]*
C:	In Corsham, Wiltshire Stan's Cafe are setting up The Black Maze early in the morning when they see a massive queue of children and parents outside a book shop.
	[LX: 37.5 Cafe acted state]

J.K.Rowling in the Cafe #2 (Success)

A:	"Would you like another cup of coffee?"
C:	"Aye make it a large frappuccino with extra whipped cream and sprinkles. Here's 20 quid, keep the fuckin' change"
A:	"Ooh thank you!" *[C punch clock]*
	[LX: 37.6]

---**2004**--

A: The United Nations declare 2004 The International Year Of Rice.
C: Hooray.
A: Facebook is launched.
C Hooray.
A: Gmail is launched.
C: Hooray.
A: Two million people join hands across Taiwan.
C: Hooray.
A: Poland, Latvia, Czech Republic, Lithuania, Estonia, Slovakia, Slovenia, Hungary, Malta and Cyprus all join the European Union.
C: Hooray.
A: Same sex marriage is legalised in Canada and Massachusetts.
C: Hooray.
A: Work begins on the construction of the Freedom Tower in NYC.
C: Hooray.
A: Greece win the Euros.
C: Really?
A: The tempera version of *The Scream* is stolen.
C: Boo.
A: Hundreds of children are taken hostage for three days in their school in Russia.
Bombs explode in the Philippines, Madrid, Egypt, Iraq, Saudi Arabia, Grozny, Prague, Jakarta.
The game World of Warcraft is released. *[A punch clock]*
And I start my BETEC *[C punch clock]* in performing arts at Kidderminster College. *[A punch clock]*
Any Stan's Cafe news for 2004?

C: Yes, James and Sarah get married and my son Robin is born at home. Sarah is one of the first people to see him. I text the team who are performing in Italy with the news that I'm a dad. My bike is stolen from the garden shed *[C punch clock] [A punch clock]*
A: Do you want to say anything else about that?
C: *[Checking clock]* No. *[C punch clock]*

--**2005**--

C: Stan's Cafe declare 2005 – 2015 the international decade of rice.
A: Hooray

A: The first parliamentary elections since 1958 are held in Iraq. Saddam Hussein goes on trial.
Steve Fossett makes the first non-stop solo un-refuelled flight around the world.
China passes a law aimed at stopping Taiwan gaining independence.
Pope John Paul II dies. Joseph Ratzinger becomes the new Pope.
MG Rover goes out of business, six thousand people lose their jobs and much of the plant is shipped to China.
[A punch clock]

Home of the Wriggler.
[LX 38: off except for map and year date]
C: *[Pedal power lights]* "From the Lickeys they look down on fields of cars,"
A: "Eerie. Massed at night, squadron by squadron"
C: "A mechanised unit, all shades of blue in the moonlight"
C: "Brian lets go of Margaret's hand"
A: "And moves for her waist. She responds in kind"
"They look beautiful don't they"
C: "Yeah, they do, but there are too many of 'em."
A: "What do you mean, I like them"
C: "There are too many of them, they're not selling. It's the wrong time of year, no one buys a car in the winter. They'll be looking to cut production, you see, there'll be a trumped up sacking and we'll be out. Cuts production and saves on wages."
A: "Margaret's not sure what to say. Brian suddenly feels stupid"
C: "Sounding like his dad"
A: "I'm getting cold"
C: "It's perishing isn't it, do you want this?"
A: "No. I think I'd like to go home"
C: "Oh, OK. I'm sorry"
A: "Brian lets go of Margaret's waist"

30

C:	"Her arm drops too. Brian can't decide if he's gone too fast"
A:	"Or messed it up talking about work"
C:	"He can't decide if it's worth trying something on in the car with the heater on"
A:	"He wishes his car had a heater"
C:	"No heater I'm afraid"
A:	"He couldn't afford it. It was that or the radio"
C:	"You may still want this"
A:	"No, I'll be fine, thank you"
C:	"She smiles"
A:	"She likes him. He should relax"
C:	"What station do you listen to? I can get Luxembourg on this"
	[LX 38.2: Map & Flip]
A:	*[A punch Clock]* Charles and Camilla marry. *[A punch Clock]*
C:	James' daughter Eve is born. She is taken to Stuttgart for the first world version of Of All The People In All The World using one hundred and four tons of rice. Robin has his first birthday there, he is passed around by members of an Indian theatre company amazed by his blond hair and blue eyes.
	[C punch clock]
A:	Live 8 Concerts take place across the world.
	{Make Poverty History}
	"The International Olympic committee has the honour of announcing that the games of the 30th Olympiad in 2012 are awarded to the city of …London."
	[A dives under the table]
	[LX 38.5: add under table light]
A:	Bombs explode in London, Sharm El Sheikh, Bangladesh, Bali and Amman.
	[LX 38.6: restore to map]
C:	*[Start peddling again]*
A:	Isabelle Dinoire becomes the first person to receive a face transplant.
	Angela Merkel becomes the first female chancellor of Germany.
	Hurricane Katrina causes death and destruction across the USA.

---2006---

A: Twitter is launched.
Paul McCartney is finally 64.
C: *[C punch clock]* Jack Trow is finally 22, gets his first paid work with Stan's Cafe performing *Of All The People In All The World* in Newcastle-upon-Tyne. *[At map]*
The show is also performed in Milan, Cork, Groningen, Norwich, Portland, Los Angeles, Bochum, Leipzig and Melbourne. Clock
[C punch clock]
A: Saddam Hussein is executed by hanging.
Serbia and Montenegro separate.
Amy Taylor fails her diving test, moves to London and starts university.
C: *[C punch clock]* Nenad Prokić is elected Member of Parliament for Belgrade. Clock! *[C punch Clock]*
A: The USA withdraws its troops from Iceland after 55 years. *[A punch clock]*
C: Stan's Cafe's rehearsal space is demolished, to make way for a library that is never built. Clock! *[A punch clock]*
A: There is a 34 day war between Israel and Lebanon.
Italy win the World Cup for the fourth time.
C: Hooray.
A: Pluto is downgraded to a dwarf planet.
C: Boo.
A: An ETA ceasefire ends with a bomb.
C: Boo.
A: The Population of the USA exceeds 300 million.
C: Hooray *[He stops peddling]*

---2007---

A: *[Using torch at table]* Russia cuts oil supplies to Poland, Germany, and Ukraine.
The Intergovernmental Panel on Climate Change release a report stating:
"Most of the observed increase in global average temperatures since the mid-20th century is very likely due to the observed increase in anthropogenic greenhouse gas concentrations."

The Cleansing of Constance Brown
[LX 38.7: Stan] [Music: Hazchem] [C in Hazchem costume]

A: In the last 26 years the world's human population has been threatened by:
HIV Aids.
Bovine Spongiform Encephalopathy.
Foot and Mouth disease.
Anthrax in letters.
Microwaves from mobile phones.
An MMR vaccine scare.
Diesel particulates.
Swine Flu.
Legionnaires Disease.
Sarin on the Tokyo Metro and in Syria.
H5N1 Avian Flu.
MRSA.
SARS.
Ebola.
And Zika.
Small Pox has been eradicated.
Malaria is still a problem .
Polio has nearly gone but the race is on to find a new antibiotic.
[A punch clock]
[Music: out]
[LX 39: General]

C: Marie Zimmerman commits suicide.
A: Who's she?
C: A friend.
A: That's sad.
C: On tour in Los Angeles Graeme gets a tattoo.
A: What of?
C: It's a drawing…it's too difficult to explain *[Depresses clock]* {Poster to find Madelaine McCann} Madelaine McCann disappears in Portugal.

A: There is a heatwave across Europe and President Pervez Musharraf declares a state of emergency in Pakistan.
Live Earth concerts take place across the world to raise awareness about climate change.
Northern Rock customers queue up to take their money out of the bank after it was unable to raise money and repay loans.
Boris Yeltsin dies and the final Harry Potter book is published.
C: "A've nailed it!"
A: I pass my driving test.

---2008---

A: It's the International Year Of The Potato.
C: Hooray.
A: 160 sq miles of Antarctica's Wilkins ice shelf disintegrates.
C: Boo.
Bill Gates steps down as Chairman of Microsoft to concentrate on philanthropic works.
C: Hooray.
A: Fidel Castro resigns as President of Cuba and is replaced by his brother.

The price of oil tops $100 a barrel for the first time.
Stock markets fall across the world. *[A punch clock]*

C: Gerard leaves Bucarest performances of The Cleansing of Constance Brown to be with his mother Constance, who dies a few days later. My mum has a hip replacement. *[C punch Clock]*

A: In a referendum the people of Ireland vote to reject the Treaty of Lisbon intended to "enhance the efficiency and democratic legitimacy of the European Union".

At the Summer Olympics in Beijing the opening ceremony features 15,000 performers, the closing ceremony features Boris Johnson.

C: *[C punch clock]* Stan's Cafe perform *Of All The People In All The World* in New York City, yards from the site of the World Trade Center, within sight of The Statue of Liberty and Ellis Island. *[C punch clock]*
[LX 39.5: Speech spot]

A: "If there is anyone out there who still doubts that America is a place where all things are possible, who still wonders if the dream of our founders is alive in our time, who still questions the power of our democracy, tonight is your answer." Barack Obama is elected 44th President of the United States.
[LX 39.6: General]

There is a political crisis in Canada following the killing of a student by police.
There are riots across Greece.
Pirates attack cargo ships off the coast of Somalia.
Lehman Brothers files for bankruptcy. {Cap Greed}
The Dow Jones Index loses 500 points in one day.
Bernard Madoff is arrested for running a Ponzi scheme that defrauded thousands of investors. 2009.
[Craig flips]

--**2009**--

A: Russia cuts gas.
Gaza wars.
Australian bush fires.
Iceland bankrupt. *[A punch clock]*

The Just Price of Flowers

[Music: Freddie (instrumental) from The Just Price of Flowers]
[LX 40: Stan's Cafe]

C: "Mr. Van Driver, may I have someone get you something, a drink perhaps, hot, cold, stiff?"
A: "No thank you. Please say what it is you have to say?"
C: "Your pension. You do understand how it works don't you. It was all explained to you by my father when your first began was it not"
A: "What?"
C: "That this final payment sum is not guaranteed, it relies on the market. It pays what the market rate is at the time of maturity, unless you choose to extend that point"
A: "And the time of maturity is next month"
C: "Yes and at this time the market is particularly weak, the weakest I can recall. If you cash in next month I fear you will get very poor returns"
A: "But, I don't understand, I've been buying a pension not investing in the tulips madness"
C: "What do you think I've been doing with your money to try and get the growth you need?"
[Music: Out and Drone in]
[LX 41: General]
A: *[A punch Clock]* Satellites collide.
Nuclear tests in North Korea.
Michael Jackson's dead.
Water on the moon.
Lisbon Treaty passed. *[A punch clock]*
And I move back to Stourbidge *[C punch Clock]* to start teaching at Kidderminster College. *[A punch clock]*

C: Stan's Cafe find a new home in the A E Harris metal working factory, one of their first acts is to stage a twenty four hour Scalextric race.

C: My second child Sorrel is born a week after Jake and Jo's first child Molly, she is taken on tour to Toronto, where Nina West marries her long time girlfriend Jane Webster in the City Hall. Company designer Simon Ford has already emigrated there. Newly recruited stage manager Billy Hiscoke likes the city so much he decides to emigrate there too, and does.
[C punch clock]

---**2010**---

A: Earthquake, tsunami, volcanic ash.
The Deepwater Horizon.
Greece's economy down the toilet.
Anti-government protests.
Miners rescued.
Spain win the World Cup.
C: Hooray.
A: West Brom are promoted.
C: Hooray.
A: They start building the new Library Of Birmingham.
[A punch Clock]
C: I'm cutting it. *[C punch Clock]*

A: Wikileaks.
 The last print edition of Encyclopaedia Britannica.
 The EU bails out Ireland.
 [A punch Clock]
C: I take Robin to his first football match.
 Amy Taylor auditions to perform Home of the Wriggler…
 … and tours with us to Beijing.
A: Yes!
 [C punch clock]
A: The Arab Spring.

---**2011**---

A: Fukushima.
 Bin Laden is killed.
 Occupy Wall. {WE are the 99%}
 There are riots in British cities. *[A punch clock]*
C: This prompts Bernadette Russell to start her 366 Days of Kindness project. *[C punch clock]*
A: Civil war in Libya. Gaddafi killed.
 Emergency in Bahrain.
 Famine in Somalia.
 Syrians flee homeland.
 ETA ends violence.
 Will and Kate marry.
 {Check Mate Kate, you've taken the king}
C: Hooray.
A: Birmingham City win the League Cup/
C: Really?
A: /and are relegated.
C: Hooray.
 [A frowns at C]
C: Boo.
 [A punch clock]
C: *Of All The People In All The World* is performed in Buenos Aries for a food bank charity.
 Cleansing Of Constance Brown is revived in Birmingham and Potsdam close to the bridge where spies were exchanged in the Cold War.
 Alia Alzougbi devises the *Cardinals* with Stan's Cafe but her Syrian passport means she can't go to the premiere in Montpellier, so her role is taken by former teenager Rochi

	Rampal who is sick in the wings.

Rampal who is sick in the wings.
The Commentators commentate on The World Gurning Championships in Egremont and succeed in not getting beaten up.

A: 2012. *[Craig flips]*

---**2012**--

A: Iran sanctions.
Greek bailout.
Diamond Jubilee {Jubliation}. Transit of Venus.
Higgs Bosun, car on Mars. Felix Baumgarten.
[A punch clock]
Anything?

C: *Just Price of Flowers* at Latitude, twelve minute long opera, Prince Charles sees the rice at the RSC, but no one's allowed to see him seeing it.

---**2013**--

C: Nina's wife Jane dies. Amy buys her first house with her partner Dan.
Nenad Prokić leaves politics and few weeks later he is invited to the premiere of *The Anatomy of Melancholy* at Warwick Arts Centre.
The Commentators are invited to star in celebrations opening of the new Library of Birmingham. *[C punch clock]*

A: *[A punch clock]* Two middle aged men pretending to be sports commentators are upstaged teenage Nobel Laurette Malala Yousafzai who opens the new Library of Birmingham.

C: Fair enough. *[C punch clock]*
A: I'm cutting it *[A punch clock]*
[LX 41.5: Acted scene table]
C: Edinburgh
"I think Exodus Steps is going to work really well"
A: "What can I get you gentlemen?"
C: "Two coffees please"
A: *[Sitting]* "So we'll see you in Los Angeles" *[Shake hands]*
C: "Fantastic, thanks Jordan"

A: *[Standing]* "here are your coffees"
C: "Thank you, here's £4, keep the change" *[C punch clock]*
    [LX 41.6: General]
A: It's the Year of Quinoa.
C: Boo.
A: Russia meteor.
    Scientists grow ear.
    Thatcher dies.
    Croatia joins EU.
    Cyprus bailout.
    Bombs, Bombs, Bombs.
    Military coup.
    Pope resigns, cardinals gather
C: *[In Cardinals costume]* "My brothers"
A: I'm cutting it!

---2014---

A: There's a crisis in Ukraine, Russia moves into Crimea.
    Plane shot down.
    [Music: Cross fade to Hex from Voodoo City]
    [LX 42: Stan's Cafe DS]
C: "The Archival Library has burnt down and with it the evidence of crimes. And Bosnia is still the mirror of Europe! Like Ukraine! For the first time since the fall of the Berlin Wall capitalism feels fear, which it needs so much to rein in its insatiable appetite. Long live the balance of fear! Without it, that immense capitalist mouth devours even what it cannot digest. We make up for the absence of ideology with the ideology of borders. Here we are, we are returning to the borders defined at the Potsdam Congress which means that the world wars of the twentieth century, not only the first one, the second one too, were waged without any rhyme or reason! Where were we, Europe – nowhere! What did we do, Europe – nothing! War was a child's game compared to the peace that was established".
    [Music: out]
    [LX 43: General]
    Finger Trigger Bullet Gun written for Stan's Cafe by Nenad Prokić.
    [Music: Court from The Cleansing Of Constance Brown]
A: Scotland votes to stay in the UK.

	Germany win World Cup.
C:	Hooray.
A:	Nigerian girls kidnapped. {Bring Back Our Girls}
	ISIS caliphate.
	Gaza strip.
	Airstrikes over Syria.
	Cuba and US restore diplomatic relations.
C:	*Any Fool Can Start A War.* *[struggling to put a child size costume on]* What the hell?
A:	It was performed by ten year olds! *[A punch clock]*

---**2015**---

	Charlie Hebdo. {Je Suis Charlie}
	Jeremy Corbyn.
	Financial crisis.
	Bombs, bombs, bombs, bombs, bombs, bombs, bombs.
	Hajj stampede.
	More air strikes in Syria.
	Paris climate change agreement.
C:	Hooray.
A:	Spock dies.
C:	Boo.
A:	Sepp Blatter resigns.
C:	Really?
A:	*[A punch clock].*
C:	Pre-teenagers Robin Stephens and Eve Yarker tour to Warsaw with *The Cleansing of Constance Brown* as Assistant Stage Managers. On her return from performing in Warsaw, Amy decides to give up teaching and concentrate on theatre full time.
A:	Hooray!
C:	*[C punch clock]*

---**2016**---

A:	Gravitational waves.
	Brexit.
	New PM.
	Muslim mayor.
	More bombs in Brussels.
	More Olympics in Rio.

	More nuclear tests in North Korea. The last VCR is made. Castro dies. Jo Cox is killed. Trump elected.
C:	Nina West marries Teresa in Manchester. I marry Charlotte in Bimingham. Eve starts secondary school. Graeme turns 50.

---**2017**--

A:	{The end is neigh} Manchester Arena. Grenfell Tower. Raqqa. Catalonia. Hurricanes. Sexism. Brexit negotiations *[extemporise until time runs out]* *[A punch clock]*
C:	Robin starts GCSE Drama. My brother has a hip replacement. My Dad feels he won't be fit enough it to see our outdoor show *The Camp*. My bike is stolen again! Rochi becomes a mum so Amy takes her role in *Time Critical* at [Insert name of venue] on [insert date]. *[C Punch clock] [Music: Cut][LX 44: Black out]*

[LX 45: Curtain Call] [Shake hands]

[LX 45: Preset & house lights]

Original Programme Notes

25 minutes of world history vs 25 minutes of personal history

Devised by Rochi Rampal, Craig Stephens and James Yarker
Performed by Rochi Rampal and Craig Stephens
with Direction from James Yarker

This show contains moments from the following shows

Memoirs of an Amnesiac
devised by Graeme Rose and James Yarker

Canute the King
devised by Amanda Hadingue, Graeme Rose and James Yarker

Voodoo City
devised by Sarah Archdeacon, Amanda Hadingue, Ray Newe,
Graeme Rose and James Yarker

Ocean of Storms
devised by Sarah Archdeacon, Amanda Hadingue and James Yarker

The Carrier Frequency
devised by Impact Theatre Cooperative
restaged by Stan's Cafe text by Russell Hoban

Good and True
devised by Sarah Archdeacon, Amanda Hadingue
Craig Stephens, Nick Walker and James Yarker

Be Proud of Me
devised by Amanda Hadingue, Craig Stephens and James Yarker

Home of the Wriggler
devised by Heather Burton-Skinner, Amanda Hadingue, Bernadette
Russell, Craig Stephens and James Yarker
Set: Mark Anderson & Helen Ingham

The Just Price of Flowers
written by James Yarker

Finger Trigger Bullet Gun
written by Nenad Prokić

With music extracts from:

Richard Chew
Desespoire Agreable (Memoirs of an Amnesiac)
Corridor Music & Turning The Tide (Canute the King)
String Quartet (Voodoo City)

Richard Chew and Jon Ward
Hex (Voodoo City)

Jon Ward
Simple Maths

Nina West
Ocean of Storms/It's Your Film, Apollo Steps
My Name Is… (Be Proud of Me)
Court and Hazchem (The Cleansing of Constance Brown)

Graeme Miller and Steve Shill
(Carrier Frequency)

Brian Duffy
Frederick (Instrumental) The Just Price Of Flowers
Drone (No Wall, Just Doors)

Stan's Cafe
Comfort Hour (Lurid and Insane)

Warning: This show contains some swearing.
It has been made especially for tonight but
A second version is planned for future touring.

About the illustration and design

The illustrations for the covers of these books were undertaken by students at Birmingham City University as the final module of their first-year illustration course during the Spring/Summer of 2018. The images were developed through workshops using variations of the theatre-devising methods employed by Stan's Cafe but adapted and applied to the making of visual work. The resulting work was shown in the pop-up exhibition *The Something Of Somebody Something* at Stan's Cafe's venue @AE Harris in May 2018.

The design concept of the books was produced by final year Graphic Design student Aimee Chapman. These were then further developed for print in a collaborative process between Stan's Cafe and the University's Innovation Product Support Service (IPSS) which involved helping the company to select appropriate DTP software, undertaking training and selecting a suitable print on demand service.

Gareth Courage
Lecturer in Illustration
Birmingham City University

www.ingramcontent.com/pod-product-compliance
Lightning Source LLC
Chambersburg PA
CBHW071758080526
44588CB00013B/2284